RABBITS

Sandie Lee Books

Rabbits

Rabbits come in all sizes and colors. There are 8 species of rabbit and several different breeds. A rabbit is not technically a rodent. It is a mammal. Rabbits were first domesticated in the Middles Ages and have been kept as pets ever since. Rabbits have been used in stories, books and movies. The Chinese calendar even includes a year of the rabbit. In this article we are going to explore all things rabbit. So read on for some more cool and fascinating rabbit facts.

Where in the World?

Did you know wild rabbits are found in most places around the world? Rabbits will live in forests, meadows, deserts, grasslands, wetlands and also wooded areas. Some live in underground burrows (or holes). Rabbits can be found in North America, Southeast Asia, some islands of Japan, Sumatra and also southwestern Europe.

The Body of a Rabbit

Did you know rabbits can measure from 8 inches in length all the way up to 20 inches? Rabbits come in many colors like, white, grey, tan, buff and black. They have long thin ears that can stand straight up. Their short tails are commonly called, cottontails. They have small eyes and small noses.

The Rabbit's Feet

Did you know a rabbit can give a powerful kick? In fact, kicking is one of the rabbits only defenses. The back feet of a rabbit are larger than its front feet. Its back feet allow the rabbit to hop and run. In some cultures, having a rabbit's foot is considered lucky.

What a Rabbit Eats

Did you know rabbits are herbivores? Rabbits only eat vegetation. In the wild, rabbits will raid farmers' gardens to get carrots, lettuce, peas and other yummy veggies. Rabbits will also eat wild berries, herbs and some flowers and shrubs. Rabbits can be very pesky and can do a lot of damage to farm crops.

The Rabbit's Special Ability

Did you know the rabbit has excellent senses? Because rabbits are hunted by many different predators, it has developed good senses. The rabbit's eyes can see in every direction at the same time. Its large ears can pick up sound waves from a long distance away. Plus, rabbits have 100 million scent cells in their noses!

The Rabbit as Prey

Did you know rabbits are hunted by many predators? Since rabbits are quite small, they are hunted by larger land mammals like, foxes and wolves and by predatory birds, like hawks and eagles. Man also hunts rabbit for its meat, fur and feet. Some rabbits are raised specifically for meat.

Rabbit Talk

Did you know rabbits can make sounds? Even though we may think of rabbits as being silent animals, they can make sounds. Rabbits will make a soft squeal or whimper if they are annoyed. If a rabbit is growling, grunting, snorting or hissing, this means it is angry. Rabbits will also scream if they are really scared or in pain.

Mom Rabbit

Did you know a mother rabbit can have hundreds of babies over her lifetime? A female rabbit is called a doe. She is pregnant for only 30 days and can give birth from 5 to 8 babies. In the wild, a mother rabbit will find a safe den or burrow to have her babies in.

Baby Rabbits

Did you know baby rabbits are called kits? Baby rabbits are born blind, helpless and without any fur. Baby rabbits only eat twice a day, as their mother's milk is very high in nutrients. Kits grow very fast. In fact, it only takes them 2 weeks before they are moving about and exploring.

Rabbit Play

Did you know rabbits like to play? In the wild, rabbits will run and chase after one another. They also like to jump up in the air and dig holes for fun. If you have two rabbits as pets, you may notice that they like to do things together, especially chew up newspaper or cardboard.

Life of a Rabbit

Did you know rabbits can live to be 9 to 12 years-old in captivity? Since rabbits are preyed upon by many different animals, wild rabbits have a shorter lifespan than pet rabbits do. Rabbits can make great pets and can even be litterbox trained like a cat. They are quiet and clean critters to own.

The Flemish Giant

As the name suggests, the Flemish giant rabbit is the biggest of them all. This furry mammal can grow to be 20 pounds! It can be black, fawn, blue or light grey in color and measure up to 32 inches in length. This breed is very gentle, despite being huge.

The Lop-Eared Rabbit

The ears on this species of rabbit hang down instead of standing straight up. The lop-eared rabbit is a common pet. It ranges in size from 3 pounds (mini-lop) all the way up to 11 pounds (English lops). To keep them as a pet, they need companionship and plenty of room to run and play.

The Angora Rabbit

This breed of rabbit has very long fur. It looks like a giant cottonball with ears and a face. The soft fluffy fur from this rabbit is used to make wool from. But don't worry the rabbit just gets a haircut for this. Angora rabbits have their hair shaved off every 3 to 4 months. They are usually gentle and docile animals.

Quiz

Question 1: When were rabbits first domesticated?

Answer 1: The middle ages

Question 2: What is the common name for the rabbits short tail?

Answer 2: Cottontail

Question 3: The rabbit has excellent senses? Name one of them.

Answer 3: Eyes can see in many directions. Large ears pick up sounds. It has 100 million scent cells in its nose

Question 4: How many babies can a rabbit have over her lifetime?

Answer 4: Hundreds

Question 5: How big does the Flemish Giant rabbit grow?

Answer 5: Up to 20 pounds and 32 inches in length

Thank you for checking out another addition from Sandie Lee Books! Make sure to check out Amazon.com for many other great titles.